Relativity and Quantum Mechanics

Principles of Modern Physics

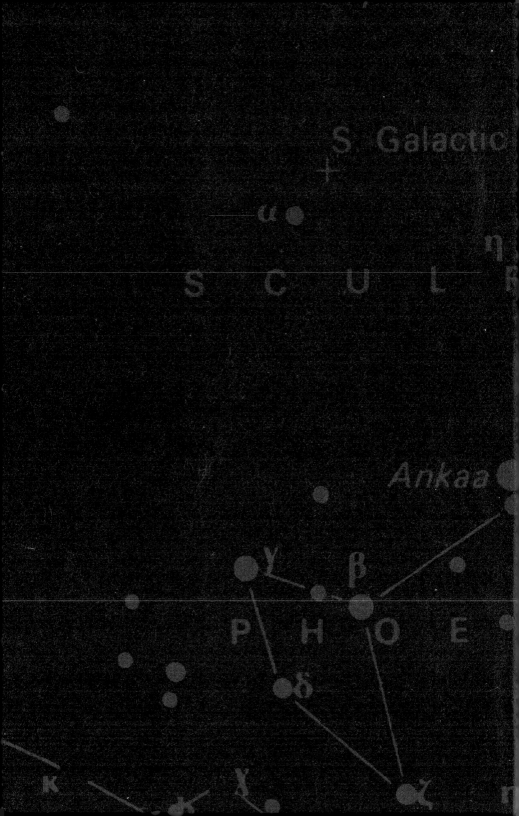

Secrets of the Universe

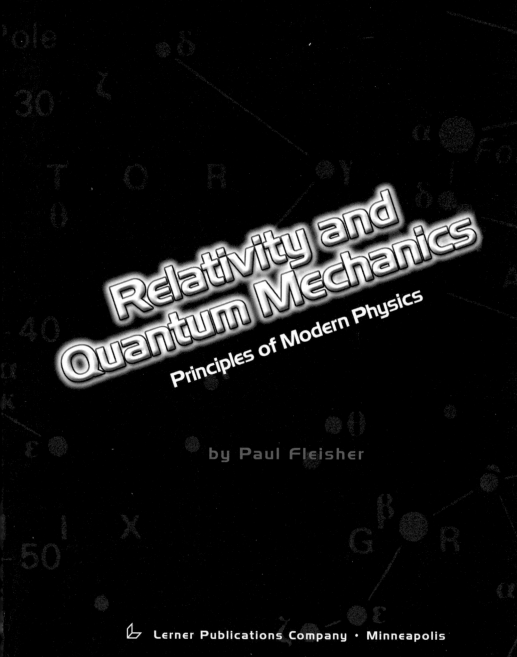

Relativity and Quantum Mechanics

Principles of Modern Physics

by Paul Fleisher

Lerner Publications Company • Minneapolis

For India

The text for this book has been adapted from a single-volume work entitled *Secrets of the Universe: Discovering the Universal Laws of Science,* by Paul Fleisher, originally published by Atheneum in 1987. Illustrations by Tim Seeley were commissioned by Lerner Publications Company. New back matter was developed by Lerner Publications Company.

Lerner Publications Company
A division of Lerner Publishing Group
241 First Avenue North
Minneapolis, MN 55401 U.S.A.

Website address: www.lernerbooks.com

Library of Congress Cataloging-in-Publication Data

Fleisher, Paul.
     Relativity and quantum mechanics : principles of modern physics / by Paul Fleisher.
        p. cm. — (Secrets of the universe)
     Includes bibliographical references and index.
     ISBN 0-8225-2989-0 (lib. bdg. : alk. paper)
     1. Relativity (Physics)—Juvenile literature. 2. Quantum theory—Juvenile literature. [1. Relativity (Physics) 2. Quantum theory.] I. Title.
QC173.575.F54   2002
530.11–dc21   00-012110

Manufactured in the United States of America
1 2 3 4 5 6 – JR – 07 06 05 04 03 02

INTRODUCTION

Everyone knows what a law is. It's a rule that tells people what they must or must not do. Laws tell us that we shouldn't drive faster than the legal speed limit, that we must not take someone else's property, that we must pay taxes on our income each year.

What Is a Natural Law?

Where do these laws come from? In the United States and other democratic countries, laws are created by elected representatives. These men and women discuss what ideas they think would be fair and useful. Then they vote to decide which ones will actually become laws.

But there is another kind of law, a scientific law. You probably have heard about Albert Einstein's law of relativity, for example. Among other things, it tells us that nothing in our universe can go faster than the speed of light. Where did that law come from, and what could we do if we decided to change it?

The law of relativity is very different from a traffic

speed limit or a law that says you must pay your taxes. Speed limits are different in different places. On many interstate highways drivers can travel 105 kilometers (65 miles) per hour. On crowded city streets they must drive more slowly. But relativity tells us that light travels at exactly the same speed no matter where it is or where it came from. In the country or the city, in France, Brazil, the United States, or even in interstellar space, light travels at 300,000 kilometers per second (186,000 miles per second).

Sometimes people break laws. When the speed limit is 88 kph (55 mph), people often drive 97 kph (60 mph) or even faster. But what happens when you try to break the law of relativity? You can't. Here on Earth, if you accurately measure the speed of light a thousand times, it will always travel at the same rate. It will never be faster or slower.

The law of relativity doesn't apply just when people are around, either. We know that the law stays in effect whether people are watching or not. The law of relativity is a natural law, or a rule of nature. Scientists and philosophers have studied events in our world for a long time. They have made careful observations and done many experiments. And they have found that certain events happen over and over again in a regular, predictable way. You have probably noticed some of these patterns in our world yourself.

A scientific law is a statement that tells how things work in the universe. It describes the way things are, not the way we want them to be. That means a scientific law is not something that can be changed whenever we choose. We can change the speed limit or the tax rate if we think they're too high or too low. But no matter how much we want to make light go faster or slower, its speed remains the same. We cannot change it; we can only describe it. A scientist's job is to describe the laws of nature as accurately and exactly as possible.

The laws you will read about in this book are universal laws. That means they are true not only here on Earth, but elsewhere throughout the universe too. The universe includes everything we know to exist: our planet, our solar system, our galaxy, all the other billions of stars and galaxies, and all the vast empty space in between. All the evidence that scientists have gathered about the other planets and stars in our universe tells us that the scientific laws that apply here on Earth also apply everywhere else.

In the history of science, some laws have been found through the brilliant discoveries of a single person. The law of relativity, for example, is the result of Albert Einstein's great flash of individual understanding. But ordinarily, scientific laws are discovered through the efforts of many scientists, each one building on what others did earlier. When one scientist receives credit for discovering a law, it's important to remember that many other people also contributed to that discovery. Even Einstein's discovery was based on problems and questions that many other scientists had been working on for years.

Scientific laws do change, on rare occasions. They don't change because we tell the universe to behave differently. Scientific laws change only if we have new information or more accurate observations. The law changes when scientists make new discoveries that show the old law doesn't describe the universe as well as it should. Whenever scientists agree to a change in the laws of nature, the new law describes events more completely, or more simply and clearly.

Relativity is good example of this. In the 1900s, scientists had believed that they should be able to measure differences in the speed of light, depending on whether the light source—a star for example—was moving rapidly toward us or away from us. They kept trying more and more accurate experiments. But better measurements still didn't show any difference. The speed of light always measured the same 300,000 kilometers per second. Einstein finally realized that there was nothing wrong with the experiments. Instead, the speed of light was always the same no matter where or when it was measured. This idea meant that scientists had to look at many of the laws of the universe in a completely new way that seemed very different from everyday experience.

Natural laws are often written in the language of mathematics. This allows scientists to be more exact in their descriptions of how things work. For example, you've probably heard of Einstein's equation $E = mc^2$.

It's one of the most famous equations in science. But don't let the math fool you. It's simply a mathematical way of saying that mass (m), or matter, can be changed into energy (E). Writing it this way lets scientists compute the amount of energy contained in a certain amount of matter.

The science of matter and energy and how they behave is called physics. In the hundreds of years that physicists have been studying our universe, they have discovered many natural laws. In this book, you'll read about several of these great discoveries. There will be some simple experiments you can do to see the laws in action. Read on, and share the fascinating stories of the laws that reveal the secrets of our universe.

CHAPTER 1

Picture yourself riding down the road in your family's car. The speedometer says that you are traveling 80 kilometers (50 miles) per hour. But how fast are you really going? If you look out the window, you'll see the countryside moving past you at 80 kilometers per hour. But if you look at the person sitting next to you in the car, it looks as if he or she isn't moving at all. You're both sitting perfectly still. Are you really moving or not?

If you think about the situation further, it gets even more puzzling. Your car is traveling on the surface of Earth. Earth is rotating on its axis at about 1,700 kilometers (1,000 miles) per hour, and so is everything on it. Perhaps you are really moving that fast.

But wait. Earth is traveling around the Sun at a speed of 30 kilometers (about 20 miles) per second. And the solar system is moving through our galaxy at a speed of about 240 kilometers (150 miles) per second. Which is the correct speed for your car? The answer is: It depends on what you're comparing your speed to. You can't measure speed unless you choose something to measure it against. Your car's speedometer measures your speed by comparing it to the road, which it considers to be standing still.

Suppose you toss a ball up and down as you sit in your car riding down the road. You would see the ball going straight up and down. But someone standing by the roadside would see something completely different. He or she would see the ball moving forward as it goes up and down. Both of you would be correct, from your own points of view. What the ball is really doing depends on how it is being seen.

The ball appears to move differently, depending on whether you are viewing it from inside or outside the car.

The name for this idea is *relativity*. Relativity means that what you observe and measure about an event depends on your own point of view as well as the event itself. Observations are relative to the frame of reference, or viewpoint, of the observer. Relativity also applies to larger events in the universe. For example, we can tell how fast our planet is moving only if we compare it to something else. Imagine a single planet in a completely empty universe. How fast is it moving? In what direction is it going? Unless we can compare it to some other object, those questions are meaningless.

Around 1900, a young German physicist named Albert Einstein wondered about relativity. How does it affect objects traveling at very high speeds? Since light travels very fast—300,000 kilometers per second in a vacuum—Einstein wondered what light waves would look like to a person traveling at the speed of light. He realized that one possible answer might be that the light would seem to be standing still, just as the person sitting next to you in the moving car seems to be sitting still.

Einstein also realized that answer didn't make sense. Light is made of waves, and waves must move to exist. So he decided to explore another possibility. He saw that the speed of light must always be 300,000 kilometers per second, no matter how fast someone is moving when he or she observes it.

Einstein's law that the speed of light is always constant doesn't seem odd at first. But it doesn't fit our everyday, commonsense view of nature. The velocity (speed of movement in a specific direction) of everything else in our world works by addition and subtraction. For example, suppose you are riding in a car at 50 kilometers (about 30 miles) per hour. You throw an apple core out the window at 10 kilometers (about 6 miles) per hour in the direction you are traveling. The total velocity of the apple core must

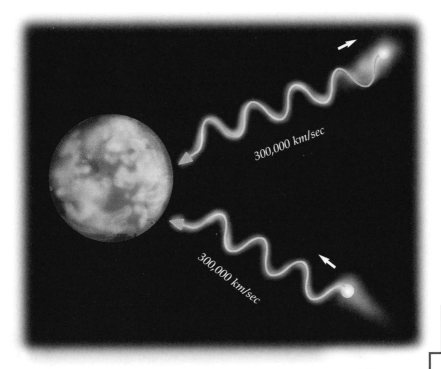

The speed of light is always the same, no matter how fast the source of the light may be moving either toward us (bottom arrow) or away from us (top arrow).

be 60 kilometers (about 36 miles) per hour. If you throw the core at 10 kph in the opposite direction, its total velocity is 40 kph (about 24 mph).

Athletes use this principle whenever they throw a ball. When a center fielder has to make a quick throw to home plate, she runs a couple of steps toward her target before she winds up and releases her throw. That way the ball has the velocity from her throwing arm plus the extra velocity of her running speed as she lets the ball go.

Imagine two stars, one moving toward Earth at 100,000 kilometers (60,000 miles) per second and one moving away at the same rate. Both stars are producing light that travels 300,000 kilometers per second. If light acted like other things in our everyday world, we would expect the light from the first star to be moving toward us at 400,000 kilometers (about 250,000 miles) per second and the light from the other to be moving toward us at 200,000 kilometers (about 120,000 miles) per second. That would seem perfectly sensible.

The trouble is, that isn't what happens. Scientists in the 1800s and early 1900s tried and tried to measure differences in the speed of light resulting from the motion of Earth and the stars. The most famous of these experiments was conducted by Albert Michelson and Edward Morley. No matter how carefully scientists designed and carried out their experiments, light always traveled 300,000 kilometers per second. It was one of the great scientific puzzles of the time.

Most physicists thought the experiments must not have been designed correctly or that the instruments used to make the measurements weren't accurate enough. But Einstein realized that the experiments had been right all along. The experimenters couldn't measure any differences in the speed of light because light always travels at the same rate. Einstein understood that this must be a basic rule of the universe.

The universal speed of light seems fairly simple. But Einstein saw that if light always travels at a constant speed, the many other rules of the universe that were considered common sense would have to change. Relativity predicts results that seem strange and very different from our everyday experiences. The mathematical calculations that explained these odd realities to Einstein are very difficult. But every one of Einstein's predictions have been proved true since his work was first published in 1905.

One of the most interesting ideas to come from Einstein's law is called *time dilation*. Time, as viewed by an outside observer, slows down as an object moves faster.

Imagine that a spaceship was zooming past Earth at 200,000 kilometers per second. If we on Earth could somehow see the clocks on that ship, they would seem to be moving much too slowly. Imagine that the people on the spaceship could see Earth at the same time. They would see our planet flashing by at 200,000 kilometers per second. Everything on their ship would seem perfectly normal to them. But from their point of view, clocks on Earth would seem much too slow!

This strange stretching out, or dilation, of time has been observed in experiments. Usually the tiny subatomic particles called muons exist for only two-millionths of a second before they disintegrate. But when they are moving near the speed of light, they last much longer. Their time is stretched out because of their speed.

Another very important part of Einstein's discovery was that energy and mass (matter) are interchangeable. Mass can be changed into energy, and energy can become matter. Relativity tells us that when an object is accelerated closer and closer to the speed of light, it gains more and more mass. This has been seen in experiments. Physicists give atomic particles, like protons or electrons, huge boosts of speed in giant particle accelerators, or atom smashers. As these particles approach the speed of light, they actually do gain more mass.

This gain in mass means that space travel at the speed of light is not possible. A scientific law discovered in the 1600s by Sir Isaac Newton, Newton's second law of motion, says that the more mass an object has, the more force is needed to accelerate it. If an object such as a spaceship gains more mass as it gets closer to the speed of light, then it will require more and more force to accelerate further. An object moving at the speed of light would have an infinite (limitless) amount of mass. That means it would require an infinite amount of force to continue to accelerate. Of course, no engine can produce infinite force. So space travelers will always have to be satisfied with slower-than-light travel.

Mass can also be changed into energy. That is exactly what happens in a nuclear reactor or a nuclear bomb. A small amount of uranium or plutonium metal is converted into energy, mostly heat and light. If this event is controlled, the heat can be used to generate electricity. If it happens all at once, it creates a huge explosion.

The part of Einstein's law that tells us that the speed of light is constant for any observer is known as *special relativity*. That's because it deals with the special case of constant, unaccelerated motion. In 1916, Einstein published another portion of his laws of relativity, known as *general relativity*. This part of Einstein's laws gives a new and better explanation for the force of gravity. General relativity tells us that there is no difference between gravity and acceleration. At least, there is no difference that we can see, feel, or measure.

Imagine yourself in an enclosed spaceship with no windows or other way of finding out what is going on in the space outside it. Your spaceship is accelerating with a constant force of 1 G (the same amount of force as Earth's gravity). When you stand on the floor of your ship, you feel your weight press down on your feet just as it would if you were on Earth. The force of the acceleration pushes you against the floor, just as you are pushed back into your seat when a car accelerates.

If you step on a scale in the spaceship, it will read the same weight as on Earth, because the force of acceleration will be pushing the floor of the ship against your body's mass. If you drop a ball, it will fall to the floor as the floor of the ship accelerates to meet it. In every way it will seem that a force is pulling everything down in the direction opposite from the ship's acceleration.

In fact, in a completely closed ship there is no way of telling whether you are accelerating through space at 1 G or just standing on a launchpad on Earth. The effects of gravity are exactly like the effects of uniform (perfectly smooth) acceleration. *Einstein's law of general relativity* tells us that from a particular point of view, there is no difference between gravity and acceleration.

Einstein's law tells us that we must think of time and space in a new way. We usually think of space as a uniform three-dimensional grid. That means that the location of every object is specified with three dimensions: length, width, and height. Relativity tells us that we must also consider a fourth dimension: time. Every object is constantly moving through a space-time continuum. To locate any object, we must say when it is as well as where it is. Like the other dimensions, measurements of time depend on your point of view. People moving at different rates will have different measurements of time!

Einstein also tells us that objects themselves affect the shape of the space-time continuum in which they are located. We can't think of space as just an empty graph-paper-like grid anymore. The shape of space and time depends on the objects in it. Very large objects such as stars have noticeable effects on the shape of space and time. A huge star actually bends or warps the shape of the space-time around it. "Straight" lines in space curve toward large masses such as planets or stars.

Try to picture space-time as a stretchy fishnet. Wherever there is a large object, the fishnet sags. Smaller objects nearby naturally roll toward the large objects. The distortions that masses cause in the shape of space-time result in what we call gravity. The force of gravity doesn't come from masses, but from the shape of space itself.

Einstein predicted that gravitation should bend even light if his laws were correct. A mass large enough to bend light is called a gravitational lens. The Sun, for example, is massive enough to bend space-time and act as a gravitational lens. The effect has been observed during eclipses.

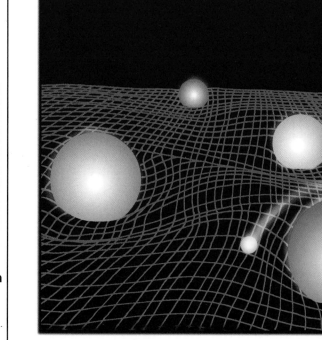

Einstein realized that large masses affect the shape of space and time.

Stars seen near the Sun during eclipses appear to be out of position, because their light has been bent by the Sun's gravity.

Relativity also predicted the existence of black holes. A black hole is a tremendously massive object formed by the collapse of a star. A black hole is so massive that it bends light back into itself. The light can never escape. Since no light ever leaves a black hole, we can never see one. But astronomers have detected huge concentrations of energy in space that are evidence of these strange objects.

The law of general relativity also showed that gravitation affects time. The closer you are to a large mass, such as a planet, the more slowly time moves.

Experiments here on Earth have shown this. Extremely accurate atomic clocks move more slowly at sea level than they do at the top of a high building. The difference in time is due to the weakening of gravity as the clock is moved farther from the center of Earth. Time slows down even more near huge objects like stars. And scientists believe that in a black hole, time stops completely!

Einstein's laws have replaced Newton's laws of motion and gravitation. Newton's laws accurately describe objects moving at comparatively low speeds. But Einstein's laws show us that objects and waves behave differently when they travel at or near the speed of light. These laws are the best description of how gravitation and motion work in our universe.

Like Newton, Einstein made many important contributions to physics. He made many of his important discoveries when he was very young. Einstein was only twenty-six years old when his first description of relativity was

The gravitational force of the Sun is strong enough to bend the light from a distant star.

published. He received many honors for his contributions to human knowledge. In 1921, he won the Nobel Prize in physics. Much of his later life was spent working for world peace. By the time of his death in 1955, he was known and respected throughout the world.

CHAPTER

Mechanics is the study of motion. It is the branch of physics that tells us how the familiar objects of our everyday world move and interact with one another. The laws of classical mechanics tell us about the motions of ordinary objects of familiar size. Whenever we see the objects in our world move, they follow the laws of classical mechanics.

Atoms and atomic particles, however, follow a different set of laws. The branch of physics that studies the structure and motion of atoms is known as *quantum mechanics*. Scientists have discovered that the laws of quantum mechanics are very different from the laws of classical mechanics.

Before 1897, when J. J. Thomson discovered the electron, scientists thought that atoms were the smallest possible pieces of matter. Thomson's discovery proved that this wasn't true. Atoms themselves were made of smaller subatomic particles. Protons, neutrons, and electrons are the three main particles that make up all atoms. Ernest Rutherford discovered the proton in the early 1900s, and the neutron was discovered by Sir James Chadwick in 1932. But dozens of other atomic particles have also been found to exist. Atoms turn out to have a complicated structure of their own. There may yet be more subatomic particles to discover.

In the early 1800s, when John Dalton first discovered that matter is made of atoms, most scientists expected atoms to follow the same rules of motion as larger pieces of matter. But an electron or a proton is nothing like a baseball or a boulder or a planet. Atomic particles don't follow the same laws that larger objects do. New laws of physics were needed to describe the behavior of electrons and other atomic particles.

The laws of quantum mechanics were written because physicists needed to describe the actions of those particles. The early part of the twentieth century was one of the most exciting times in the history of science because so many brilliant scientists were working together to solve the mysteries of how atoms work.

Quantum mechanics is one of the most important areas of modern physics. It is so different from our everyday experiences, however, that we can't do experiments with ordinary objects to show how quantum laws work. Quantum laws apply only to matter the size of atoms and smaller. To understand how quantum mechanics is different from the classical mechanics of our everyday world, try to picture the following imaginary example.

Imagine an ordinary garden hose attached to an ordinary water faucet. When you turn on the faucet just a little, a trickle of water begins to flow through the hose. A small amount of water dribbles out of the nozzle. As you gradually turn the faucet handle, more and more water flows through the hose. The nozzle gradually sprays water farther and farther. By adjusting the amount of water flowing from the faucet, you can make the water spray 0.5 meter, 1 meter, 3 meters, 4.5 meters (about 1.5, 3, 10, 15 feet), or whatever other distance you choose. That is how a hose works according to classical mechanics.

Imagine another hose. This time, as you slowly and gradually turn on the faucet, nothing happens. No water comes out of the nozzle, not even a dribble. Then, when you turn the faucet to a certain point, the hose starts spraying water. But it sprays in a very special way. The water sprays out in droplets of exactly 1 milliliter (0.03 fluid ounce) each, which land exactly 1 meter (3 feet) away.

You turn the faucet handle farther, but the hose continues to spray only at the 1-meter distance. Then, all of a sudden, the spray jumps out to a distance of 2 meters

classical garden hose

quantum garden hose

A "classical" garden hose sprays water in the ordinary way. But an imaginary "quantum" hose would only spray water drops with certain amounts of force.

(about 7 feet). None of the water lands between the 1-meter and 2-meter marks. One moment the stream reaches 1 meter, and the next it reaches 2 meters.

As you gradually increase the flow of water from the faucet, the same "jumps" keep happening. The water will spray only at whole-meter distances. And it always sprays in droplets of exactly 1 milliliter each. The spray is not continuous. Instead, the nozzle sprays only in certain predictable distances and amounts. Those amounts could be called quanta, and this odd hose would be a quantum garden hose.

Obviously, this sort of strange behavior doesn't really happen with garden hoses. But it does happen with electrons. It's called the *photoelectric effect*, and it was a great mystery to the physicists of 1900.

When light shines on certain metals, it causes an electric current. That is known as the photoelectric effect (*photo-* is the Greek prefix meaning "light"). You may have already experienced this effect without realizing it. It's what makes an electric-eye door open and close. In an electric eye, a narrow beam of light shines on a special metal plate. As long as the light is shining onto the metal receiver, electricity flows. But when someone walks by, the light is interrupted, just as it is when you put your hand between a movie projector and the screen. Interrupting the beam of light stops the flow of electricity, triggering a motor that opens the door.

The photoelectric effect is also used to generate electricity from sunlight. Special solar cells generate an electric current when light shines on them. You may have seen photoelectric cells like this on solar-powered calculators.

You might expect that the brighter the light shining on the metal, the more energy the electrons will have. But it doesn't work that way. As you increase the amount of light shining on a photoelectric cell, the amount of electrical

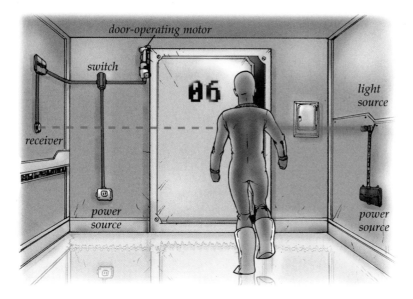

door-operating motor

switch

light
source

receiver

power
source

power
source

When the man interrupts the beam of light hitting a photoelectric cell, a switch turns on the motor, opening the door.

current produced will increase. But the voltage (or energy level) will not change. It's as if we turned up the water flow in our garden hose and more water came out of the nozzle, but it didn't spray any farther than it did when there were just a few drops flowing through the hose.

Physicists experimenting with photoelectric metals found that some light won't produce any electric current at all. For example, red light won't cause any electrons to flow, no matter how bright it is. However, even a very dim blue light will generate some electrical current. But the most surprising result was that when the brightness of the blue light is increased, the energy level of the flowing electrons stays the same.

Scientists expected the photoelectric effect to work like the classical garden hose described earlier. The more light they shone on the metal, the more voltage they expected to get. But that's not what happened. Instead, the photoelectric

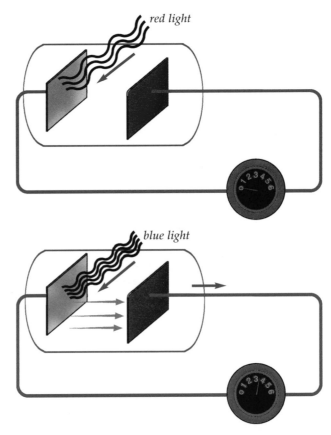

red light

blue light

Red light *(top)* will not cause a current to flow in a photoelectric cell, but blue light *(bottom)* will.

effect works like our imaginary quantum garden hose. Either you get electrons with certain specific amounts of electrical energy or none at all.

Why does electricity flow in a piece of metal just because light is shining on it? Electricity is the movement of tiny particles called electrons. How can light cause those particles to move? Why does dim blue light make electrons flow, when much brighter red light does not? And most of all, why do the electrons have only certain energy levels as they flow through the metal?

Two German scientists, Albert Einstein and Max Planck, finally solved the mystery. And with their work, quantum mechanics was born. Einstein and Planck proved that atoms and their particles—electrons, protons, and neutrons—follow different rules from the large chunks of matter that we are familiar with in our daily lives. In just a few years of rapid scientific advancement, a new set of laws about how the smallest bits of matter behave was discovered.

In 1900, Planck was studying the problem of how light radiates from a glowing object. He discovered that light waves can have only certain whole-number amounts of energy. The energy of any light wave had to be a multiple of a certain extremely small number. That number, usually represented by the letter h, is known as Planck's constant. It is a very important number. Planck's constant is the basic unit of energy in the universe, just as the speed of light is the basic speed limit.

Planck's law says that the energy of light is directly proportional to its frequency. Mathematically, it is written like this:

$$\text{Energy} = h \times \text{frequency} \quad \text{or} \quad E = h \times f$$

In Planck's equation, E is the energy of a certain wavelength of light. Planck's constant is h, and f is the frequency of the light. Frequency tells us how rapidly the light wave vibrates (the number of vibrations per second). Light waves with higher frequencies vibrate more often in a given amount of time. Higher-frequency light also has a shorter wavelength than lower-frequency light. That's because high-frequency light vibrates more often in the same distance.

Planck's equation tells us that the higher the frequency (and the smaller the wavelength) of light, the more energy it has. For example, blue light has a higher frequency than red light. So waves of blue light have more energy than waves of red light.

Planck's discovery says something else too. Light may act like a wave, but it comes only in specific amounts of energy. Light always comes in little chunks or bits. Because light energy only comes in exact amounts, it has to be considered a particle! Planck called each little chunk of light a quantum (plural: quanta).

A few years after Planck's discovery, Albert Einstein was working on the problem of the photoelectric effect. He realized that he could use Planck's discovery to explain what happens: Electrons can absorb only light waves with certain amounts of energy. The light acts like it is made of particles, not waves. Either an electron absorbs a whole

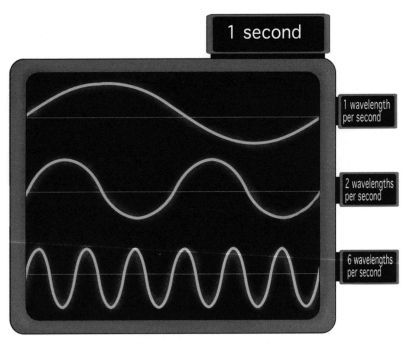

1 second

1 wavelength per second

2 wavelengths per second

6 wavelengths per second

Light waves with higher frequencies also have shorter wavelengths. If the waves are shorter, more wave crests will pass by a certain point in the same amount of time.

quantum of light or none. An electron cannot absorb part of the energy of a light particle. If the light has enough energy, it knocks the electron away from its atom and starts an electric current. If the light doesn't have enough energy, nothing happens at all.

Einstein called the light particles photons. The photons of red light simply don't have enough energy to bump the electrons away from their atoms. So no matter how much red light shines on the metal, no current will be generated. Photons of blue light have a shorter wavelength. (Remember that a higher frequency equals a shorter wavelength.) So blue photons have more energy than red photons. Blue photons are powerful enough to generate a current. That is true even in very dim light. Dim blue light has fewer photons, but each photon still has all the energy of blue light.

Max Planck received a Nobel Prize in 1918 for his discovery that light comes in whole-number amounts of energy, or quanta. Three years later, Albert Einstein won a Nobel Prize for his explanation of the photoelectric effect.

The discoveries of Planck and Einstein provided an answer to one of the longest-running scientific disputes in history: Is light a particle or a wave? In the 1600s, Isaac Newton's study of light convinced him that it is made up of many tiny particles. But Christiaan Huygens argued that light behaves like a wave. Since that time, scientists studying light have collected evidence to support each of these ideas. Most experiments showed that light behaves like a wave. But there were others that showed that light acts more like a stream of particles. Which was correct? Is light a wave or is it a particle?

Quantum mechanics has finally given us the answer. Light must be considered as both a wave and a particle. It usually behaves like a wave, but it comes in specific-sized bits, like particles.

Since the early 1900s, many more advances have been made in quantum mechanics. Modern physics explains many events that happen because of the special behavior of atoms and atomic particles.

One thing that quantum mechanics explains is how atoms combine to form chemical compounds. In 1913, the Danish physicist Niels Bohr created a picture of the atom that explained the properties of different elements. You are probably familiar with his idea of atomic structure. Bohr saw the atom as a tiny central nucleus surrounded by orbiting electrons. The nucleus is made of protons and neutrons and has a positive charge. The negatively charged electrons

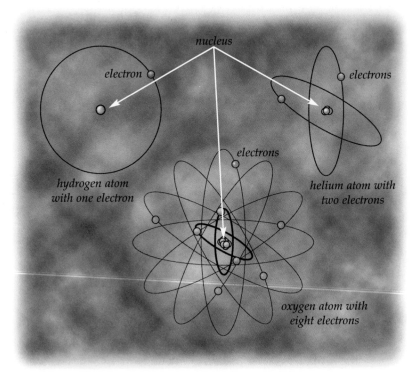

nucleus

electron

electrons

electrons

hydrogen atom
with one electron

helium atom with
two electrons

oxygen atom with
eight electrons

Bohr suggested that electrons orbit the nucleus of an atom in "shells." The oxygen atom (center) has an inner and an outer electron shell.

orbit around the nucleus in layers called shells that have different energy levels.

According to Bohr's theory, the electrons in the outermost shell of an atom can be shared with other atoms. In this way, atoms bond together to form molecules. Only the outermost electrons of any atom are free to combine with other atoms in chemical reactions.

Bohr also hypothesized that an atom can have no more than eight electrons in its outermost shell. This explained why the elements follow the pattern of properties described in Russian scientist Dmitri Mendeleyev's periodic table. Mendeleyev's arrangement of atoms has eight basic families. The elements in each family all have the same number of electrons in their outer shells. For his contributions to the understanding of atomic structure, Bohr received a Nobel Prize in 1922.

But Bohr's idea was just the beginning. Physicists continued to improve their description of how the atom works. Although electrons and other parts of atoms are usually thought of as particles, they often behave like waves. In the mid-1920s, Prince Louis-Victor-Pierre-Raymond de Broglie and Erwin Schrödinger showed that electrons vibrate around the atom in a pattern of waves. What Bohr called orbits were actually wave patterns. Only certain wave patterns fit around the nucleus of each atom.

Other atomic particles act like waves as well. In the world of the atom, it's impossible to distinguish between waves and particles. Light can be a particle, and electrons are matter-waves!

Each kind of atom has a certain number of precise wave patterns its electrons can follow. An electron jumps to a higher-energy wave pattern when it absorbs a photon of energy. It emits, or sends out, a photon of light when it jumps back to a lower energy level. There are no positions between the two energy levels. The electron occupies either one level or the other, with no stops in between.

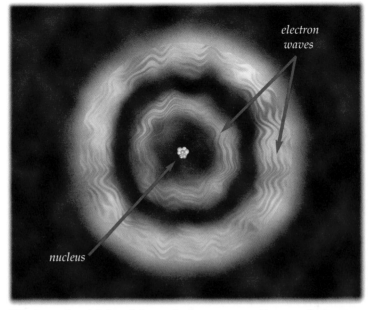

Modern physicists picture electrons as patterns of waves vibrating around the atomic nucleus.

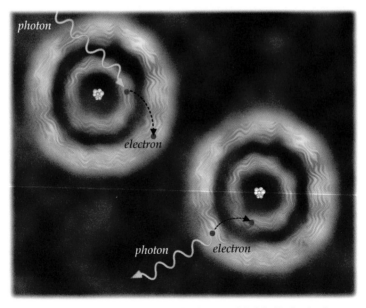

When atoms absorb or emit photons of light, their electrons "jump" from one energy level to another.

This jump between energy levels is sometimes known as a quantum leap. The energy that an electron emits as light must equal the amount of energy it absorbs from photons. So the total amount of energy stays the same.

As an element gets hot, it radiates energy in the form of light. For example, the gases in a candle flame are hot enough to give off yellow light. The gases in our Sun also glow brightly, giving off tremendous amounts of light energy.

Each chemical element radiates light only at certain wavelengths. That's because the atoms of each element have their own special arrangement of electron wave patterns. Each element has its own unmistakable set of wavelengths that it produces as it glows. Because of this, the light that elements give off when heated can be used to identify them.

The instrument that scientists use to examine the spectrum of light is called a spectroscope. If you shine the light from a glowing gas through a spectroscope, it breaks up into all the different wavelengths of light being emitted by the gas. Since each element has its own special set of wavelengths, a spectroscope can be used to identify all the elements in a sample of glowing gas.

Spectroscopes are so sensitive that they can even recognize the elements in the light of a distant star. In fact, the element helium wasn't discovered here on Earth. It was first found in the spectrum of the Sun viewed through a spectroscope. By examining the spectra of stars, scientists can see that the very same elements found on Earth are also found throughout the universe. This means that the same physical and chemical laws that apply here on Earth must apply everywhere else in the universe as well.

Quantum laws also explain what happens inside the fluorescent lightbulbs in your home. Fluorescent lightbulbs are filled with a gas. When electric current flows through the gas, it boosts the energy of some of the electrons in the atoms of gas. The electrons emit photons as they vibrate with the added energy. Those photons hit a special coating on the inside surface of the lightbulb. Electrons in this coating absorb these photons and then re-emit them as the visible light we see.

To summarize the rules of quantum mechanics:

- The laws of motion that apply to large objects do not apply to atomic particles.
- The smaller the wavelength of light, the more energy it has.
- Energy (including light) always comes in specific-sized bits, which we call quanta or photons.
- Light acts like a particle as well as a wave.
- Electrons and other subatomic particles act like waves as well as particles.

CHAPTER 3

Conservation of Mass/Energy

Whenever changes take place in our universe, certain things must remain constant. The laws that tell us what remains constant are known as the laws of conservation.

In the late 1700s, Antoine-Laurent Lavoisier proved that when substances change form in chemical reactions, the total amount of mass must still remain the same. That law is known as the *law of conservation of matter*. In the mid-1800s, James Prescott Joule proved that energy could be converted from one form to another, but the total amount of energy in any reaction always remains the same. That law is known as the *law of conservation of energy*.

In the early 1900s, however, Albert Einstein gave scientists a new understanding of matter and energy. This new viewpoint was found in Einstein's most famous equation:

$$E = mc^2$$

You have almost certainly heard of or seen this equation. But you may not know what it means. Einstein's equation is read: "E equals *mc* squared." *E*, in this equation, stands for energy, *m* stands for mass, and *c* is the speed of light. Squaring a number means multiplying it by itself.

This little equation is a mathematical way of stating a very big idea. It says that matter and energy are actually different forms of the same thing! Matter can be converted into energy and energy can be converted into matter. In a way, you could think of all the matter in our universe as frozen energy.

Pick up a pencil or a match, or look at your little finger. Whatever piece of matter you look at is composed of billions of tiny atoms. Each atom is vibrating with energy. Energy holds the atoms in place. Energy connects the atoms with one another to form molecules. And energy even holds the tiny subatomic particles together to form the atoms themselves. Each atom is a whirling, pulsing clump of energy we call matter.

Einstein's equation tells us that there is a tremendous amount of energy locked up in even the tiniest bits of matter. The equation tells us how to figure out how much energy (*E*) there is in a piece of matter. We must multiply the amount of matter (*m*) by the speed of light (*c*) squared.

The speed of light is a very large number. Squaring the speed of light gives us an enormous number. If we could somehow release all the energy in a single gram of matter, we would have a tremendous amount of energy. One gram of matter is equal to more than 21 billion calories of energy. That is the amount of energy released by burning 2,700 metric tons (3,000 tons) of coal!

Einstein's equation also tells us that if we gave an object more energy, we could increase its mass. To do this, we would have to add tremendous amounts of extra energy. You may be wondering if these events are actually possible.

Could we really change a piece of matter into energy? Could we somehow turn energy into matter? The answer is yes. Both things have been done here on Earth during the last fifty years.

Scientists have changed energy into mass in giant particle accelerators that are used in modern physics research. A particle accelerator is a huge machine that boosts the speed of tiny atomic particles almost to the speed of light. These accelerators are circular tubes, sometimes miles around. Atomic particles are held in these tubes and speeded up with electromagnetic force. Powerful magnets keep the particles from flying out through the walls of the tube. The atomic particles, such as protons or electrons, whirl around the ring of tubes at enormous speeds. The tubes have no air in them, and so the particles have no atoms to collide against. Each time they zoom around the ring they are given another boost of power from an electromagnetic field. They go a little faster with each boost.

After they've traveled around the tube millions of times and received millions of energy boosts, the particles are traveling at almost the speed of light. Because of their speed, they have tremendous energy. The beam of particles is then aimed at a target. Of course, the atomic particles are much too fast and much too small to see. So physicists find out about them by examining the evidence they leave behind when they hit the target. Researchers can keep a careful photographic record of what happens to the target as the particles hit.

Imagine that you arrive at the scene of an accident. A vehicle has crashed into a wall, but the vehicle has been taken away. You know the vehicle that hit the wall was moving at 50 kilometers (about 30 miles) per hour. It should be easy for you to tell whether the vehicle was a bicycle, a small car, or a large truck. Just look at how much damage has been done. A truck will certainly cause much more destruction than a bicycle.

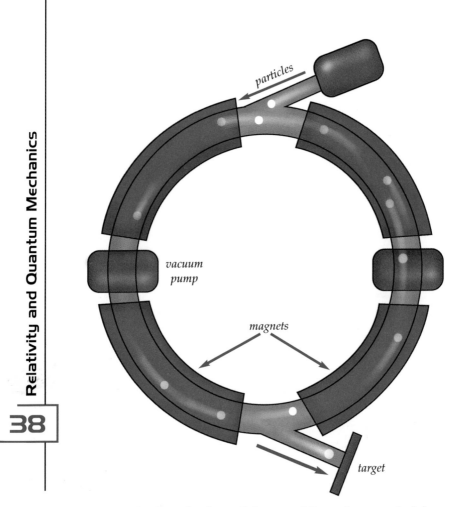

In an accelerator, atomic particles speed through an empty tube, controlled by many magnets. When they are moving fast enough, the particles are directed toward a target.

Scientists study the results of the collisions in their accelerators in a similar way. They can't see the speeding particles, but they know how much energy the particles were given as they were accelerated. The scientists can study the evidence that the collisions of the particles left behind. For example, from studying photographs of very fast protons hitting their targets, scientists can tell that these particles have more mass than ordinary protons. The energy that they received as they accelerated to tremendous speeds has been converted into extra mass. So particle accelerators have actually managed to turn tremendous amounts of energy into tiny bits of matter.

What about turning matter into energy? That has been done too, in nuclear reactors and nuclear bombs. A nuclear bomb uses about 10 kilograms (20 pounds) of uranium or plutonium metal for fuel. In a nuclear reaction, the atoms of fuel split apart, forming atoms of other elements. When an atom splits, some of its mass is released as energy. When a nuclear bomb explodes, about 1/1000 of its nuclear fuel is converted from matter into energy. So a small atomic bomb explodes with the force of only 10 grams (0.4 ounces) of matter! But the energy in that small amount of matter creates the enormous explosion and blast of the bomb.

The same conversion of matter into energy takes place in a nuclear reactor. In a reactor, the conversion from matter to energy is carefully controlled to avoid an explosion. The radioactive fuel in a nuclear reactor is extremely dangerous to handle. But suppose you could weigh the fuel that's put into a reactor, allow it to run for a year, and then weigh the fuel again. You would find that a small fraction of the weight had disappeared. Some of the uranium in the reactor would have been converted to the heat that is then used to generate electricity. But even in a nuclear reactor or in a tremendous nuclear explosion, mass is not completely converted to energy. Only a small portion of the energy frozen in the matter is released as energy. The rest remains in the form of atoms and atomic particles.

The Sun also changes mass into energy. The Sun is a giant nuclear reactor, constantly transforming part of its mass into energy. We receive some of that energy here on Earth as sunlight.

You can even see mass transformed into energy right before your eyes. Just light a match. Tiny quantities of mass are converted to energy even in ordinary chemical reactions. When a match burns, a minute amount of the match's mass is released as energy. We see that energy as light and heat. But the amount of mass that becomes energy is so tiny that not even the most sensitive scale could measure it.

Einstein's equation shows that mass can be changed into energy and that energy can be changed into mass. We can no longer say that the total amount of mass still remains the same in every reaction. Some mass is lost, becoming energy. And we can no longer say that the total amount of energy in any reaction always remains the same. Some energy may be converted into mass! The law of conservation of matter and the law of conservation of energy are not quite true. Matter and energy are equivalent. Matter is simply energy in a different form. So we must combine the two laws into one. Scientists now use the *law of conservation of mass/energy*. It says that the total amount of mass and energy in any reaction must remain the same. Mass may be converted to energy or energy may be converted to mass, but no mass or energy can be created or destroyed.

All those changes came from Einstein's simple little equation: $E = mc^2$. It has given us a whole new way of looking at our universe and ourselves.

CHAPTER 4

The instruments of science have become better and better over the past four hundred years. Scientific measurements have become more and more accurate. In the early 1900s, it seemed as if anything scientists wanted to know could be measured. It was just a matter of making a measuring device that was accurate enough and then using it to look at whatever was to be measured. At that time, what scientists most wanted to look at were atomic particles.

In studying a moving object, you need two pieces of information. You need to know the object's current location and its momentum. Momentum is a measurement of the amount of motion of an object. It includes both the object's mass and its velocity. If you know an object's location and its momentum, you can then predict what it will do as it continues its motion. Picture a bowling ball rolling down an alley. Suppose that at a particular moment you know exactly where it is. You also know exactly how fast it's moving and in what direction. If you know these things, you can predict exactly where the ball will hit when it reaches the end of the alley.

In the early 1900s, scientists wanted to find out exactly what was happening inside an atom. How fast did the electrons move, and exactly where were they located in an atom? Just as for measuring any other moving object, physicists needed two pieces of information about an electron. They needed to know its position and its momentum.

Think about what actually happens when we look at something. First of all, we need a source of light. This might be a lamp or a flashlight or the Sun. Light waves from our light source hit the object we are observing and bounce back to our eye. Our eye senses the light that hits it and sends an image to our brain.

The same thing happens when we take a picture with a camera. We still need an object to observe, a light source, and a piece of film to record the image. As a rule, to make any observation we must have three things: an object to observe, some light to bounce off the object, and an observing instrument, like an eye or a camera.

If you look at something large, like a chair or a tree or a dog, shining a little light on it doesn't affect it very much. But something strange happens when you try to look at an electron. Suppose we try to look at an electron with ordinary light.

Visible light has a wavelength about ten thousand times larger than the width of an atom. And a single electron is much, much smaller than a whole atom. When we try to see an electron by hitting it with ordinary light, we find that it is impossible. The light waves are so much larger than the electron that we can't get any picture at all. They simply miss the target. We can get no idea of where the electron is or how fast it is moving.

But perhaps we can see an electron if we use a different kind of light. To get a clearer picture of the electron, we need to use light with a much smaller wavelength. That way, the light waves won't miss the electron so badly. Instead, they will bounce off the electrons and come back to be recorded on a camera. X rays and gamma rays have much smaller wavelengths than visible light. They can also be used to take a photograph. Why not shine X rays on an electron and take a picture of its location that way?

But there's a problem—X rays and gamma rays have very high energy. Planck showed that the energy of light increases as its wavelength decreases. X rays are so very powerful that when one of these light waves hits an electron,

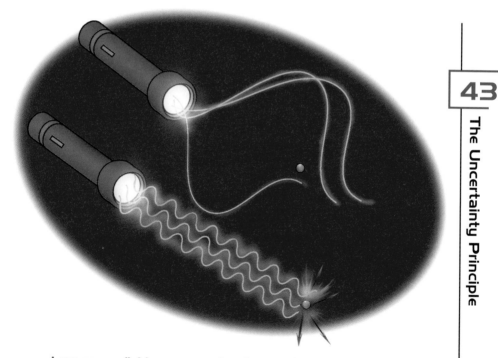

Low-energy light waves are too large to locate an atomic particle like an electron. High-energy light waves hit the particle hard enough to knock it away in unpredictable directions.

it knocks it completely off course. It totally changes the electron's speed and direction. The X ray may bounce back to a camera and tell us where the electron was at the moment when it was hit. But there is no way to predict where it is now and where it's going.

Looking at an electron with X rays is a little like trying to find out where a golf ball is by throwing tennis balls at it. Imagine that you are in a completely dark room. You know that somewhere in front of you is a golf ball. You have a supply of tennis balls. You toss the tennis balls out into the dark, keeping careful track of where you throw each one. Eventually one of your tennis balls hits the golf ball squarely and bounces right back to you. You know where the golf ball was when you made your throw. But where is it now? You have no idea. In locating the golf ball, the tennis ball has knocked it away somewhere. You can only guess where it might have gone.

When we look for electrons with very high-energy light waves, we can get a sharper picture of an electron's location. But just by observing the electron, we have caused a change in its momentum. Atomic particles cannot be observed without disturbing them. That means there must always be some uncertainty about where atomic particles are and what they are doing. We will never be able to know everything about an electron or a proton or a neutron. They will always look fuzzy to us.

This law, discovered by Werner Heisenberg in 1927, is known as the *Heisenberg uncertainty principle*. The uncertainty principle can be stated like this: It is impossible to measure atomic particles without disturbing the particles. Therefore it is never possible to know everything there is to know about these particles.

Perhaps this is not surprising, since atomic particles are wavelike in their behavior. De Broglie and Schrödinger showed that electrons can best be thought of as matter-waves vibrating around the nucleus of an atom. We wouldn't expect a wave to have a single fixed position. Atoms are often pictured as miniature solar systems, with electron "planets" orbiting a nucleus "Sun." But the uncertainty principle reminds us that this is only a picture to help us get an idea of something that is impossible to see. An atom is not a miniature solar system. Its actions follow a different set of rules. The most accurate picture of an atom that we can imagine is a fuzzy set of probable locations and velocities for the atom's particles. These locations and speeds are only likely—not certain.

The Heisenberg uncertainty principle is a very important idea. It tells us that no matter how accurate or careful our scientific measurements become, we can never know everything about the universe. If nothing else, there will always be uncertainty about the actions of atomic particles. We can never be sure what they are doing at any given time. The best that physicists can do is to determine where an electron is most likely to be at any time, and how fast it is most likely to be moving.

Heisenberg's uncertainty principle is a law that applies to the actions of atomic particles. But the idea is an important one for other sciences too. All scientists need to remember that the process of observing something often has an effect on the thing that they are observing. Therefore, it may be impossible to observe any event in perfectly natural, undisturbed conditions.

For example, biologists often look through a microscope at tiny creatures in a drop of water. But the very act of looking at those creatures can change the creatures' behavior. They have been removed from their environment and placed in a single drop of water on a glass slide. A microscope focuses extra light on the subjects being observed so that they can be seen clearly. The light also raises the temperature of the water. All these changes may affect the actions of the creatures the biologist is observing.

Suppose we wanted to study the activities of forest animals, without the interference of human beings. We could set up an automatic camera in the woods and then leave. Even so, the strange appearance of the camera and its whirring sound might affect the animals' behavior in unexpected ways. Perhaps the scent of the camera or the humans who set it up might also affect what the animals do. No matter how careful we were, we could never be certain that the animals we photographed were behaving in a completely natural way.

Here's one more example from everyday life. Suppose your mother wanted to see how your little brother behaves in kindergarten class. So she decides to visit his class for a couple of hours and watch him work and play. Would you expect your brother's behavior to be exactly the same as it would be if your mother weren't there? Of course not. Even if your mother just sits quietly and watches, your brother will know that she is watching him. Because she's watching, he might be especially careful about behaving well. Or he might decide to show off to get her attention. Just the fact that your mother is present will affect what she sees.

Heisenberg's uncertainty principle tells us it is impossible for science to understand the universe completely. No matter how carefully we experiment, no matter how accurate our scientific instruments are, some things in the universe will always be hidden from us. In an effort to find the laws that tell us how our universe works, scientists will continue to experiment. But in a sense, Heisenberg's uncertainty principle may be the last law of the universe. No matter how wonderful human brains may be, we can't know everything.

But that doesn't mean that we know all that we can know about the universe. Scientists still have much to learn about the stars and planets, the atom, and the miracles of life. There are still more laws to discover and many more mysteries to solve. Perhaps you may one day add your name to that distinguished list of scientists who have helped discover the secrets of the universe.

Relativity and Quantum Mechanics

48

1675	Olaus Rømer proves that the speed of light is finite
1678	**Christiaan Huygens proposes his wave theory of light**
1687	Isaac Newton publishes his *Principia*
1692	Witchcraft trials take place in Salem, MA
1704	**Isaac Newton publishes *Opticks*, including his particle theory of light**
1773	Boston Tea Party
1775–1783	American War of Independence
1787	U.S. Constitution is signed
1799	The Rosetta Stone is discovered in Egypt
1808	**John Dalton publishes his theory that all elements are made up of atoms**
1828	Noah Webster's *American Dictionary of the English Language* is published
1829	Louis Braille's system of writing for the blind is first published (revised in 1837)
1849	Armand Fizeau makes an accurate measurement of the speed of light
1859	Charles Darwin publishes *On the Origin of Species by Means of Natural Selection*
1861–1865	American Civil War
1865	President Abraham Lincoln is assassinated
1876	Alexander Graham Bell patents the telephone

1887	Albert Michelson and Edward Morley conduct their experiments on the speed of light
1897	J. J. Thomson discovers the electron
1900	Max Planck discovers Planck's law and Planck's constant
1903	The Wright brothers make the first manned airplane flight
1905	Albert Einstein publishes his special theory of relativity, including $E=mc^2$
1908	Henry Ford begins production of the Model T
1913	Niels Bohr presents his model of the atom
1914–1918	World War I
1916	Albert Einstein publishes his general theory of relativity
1919	Ernest Rutherford discovers the proton
1924	Louis de Broglie proposes that particles, such as electrons, can act like waves
1927	Werner Heisenberg states his uncertainty principle
1932	James Chadwick proves the existence of the neutron
1939–1945	World War II
1945	First atomic bomb is exploded in New Mexico; the United States drops atomic bombs on Hiroshima and Nagasaki, Japan
1964	Murray Gell-Mann proposes a theory of quarks (subatomic particles)
1979	Nuclear accident at Three Mile Island, Pennsylvania
1986	Nuclear accident at Chernobyl, Ukraine

Niels Bohr (1885–1962) was a Danish theoretical physicist. He was one of the scientists who helped solve the mystery of how electrons behave. In 1913, Bohr proposed a new explanation of electron orbits. In Bohr's model of the atom, electrons occupy specific energy levels but are able to "hop" from level to level under certain conditions. This theory combined ideas of classical physics with those of quantum physics and was a very important step in understanding the structure of the atom. Bohr also led an eventful life beyond this discovery. Among other accomplishments, he won a Nobel Prize in physics, escaped Nazi-occupied Denmark in a fishing boat, and worked with other scientists to research the dangers of the atomic bomb.

Prince Louis-Victor-Pierre-Raymond de Broglie (1892–1987) was a French physicist. His colorful family history included a great-great-grandfather who had been guillotined during the French Revolution. De Broglie graduated from college with a degree in history, but he began seriously studying science after serving at the Eiffel Tower radio station during World War I. Intrigued by the work of Max Planck and Albert Einstein, de Broglie concentrated his studies on theoretical physics. He won a Nobel Prize in physics for his revolutionary theory that, just as light waves could act like particles, particles such as electrons could display wavelike properties. Later in his life, de Broglie worked as a professor of physics and published many scientific articles and books.

James Chadwick was a British physicist who was
(1891–1974) extremely dedicated to his science. In
1913, after studying in Manchester
and Cambridge, England, he received a scholarship to
work with a researcher in Berlin, Germany. When World
War I began in 1914, Chadwick was captured as a foreign-
er and held in a horse stable for four years. Even under
these circumstances, Chadwick tried to study as much as
he could. His hard work paid off, and in 1932 he proved
the existence of the neutron. Following this discovery,
which won him a Nobel Prize, Chadwick became a professor in Liverpool, England. During World War II, he was
one of many scientists who traveled to the United States to
help develop the atomic bomb.

John Dalton was a British scientist who began teach-
(1766–1844) ing when he was just twelve years old.
He is best known for developing the
theory that substances are composed of atoms. His interests
were broad, ranging from meteorology to color blindness.
Color-blind himself, Dalton even requested that his eyes be
donated to scientific research after his death. In the area of
meteorology, he was particularly interested in rainfall and
atmospheric humidity. This interest may have been a result
of the time he spent living in England's rainy Lake Country.
Beginning in 1787 and continuing until his death, Dalton
kept a daily journal of weather observations, recording a
total of about 200,000 entries. Dalton also studied gases,
contributing to the theory that was eventually formulated
in Charles's law.

Albert Einstein was a German physicist. As a student,
(1879–1955) he enjoyed reading but disliked lec-
tures and tests, and he was never a
particular favorite with his teachers. His undistinguished
university record led him to a job as a clerk in a Swiss

patent office. From these modest beginnings he went on to introduce the theory of relativity, one which changed the world of physics forever. An international figure, Einstein was named a public enemy by the Nazis in Germany, acted as an unofficial adviser to U.S. president Franklin D. Roosevelt on the threat of the atomic bomb, and was even offered the presidency of Israel. In his private life, however, he had simple, quiet tastes. His hobbies included music and sailing.

Werner Heisenberg (1901-1976) was a German physicist. A brilliant mathematician, he was important in continuing the work that Einstein and others had begun in the field of quantum theory. Heisenberg is best known for his uncertainty principle. He introduced this revolutionary theory when he was only twenty-six years old. In his private life, he enjoyed activities from mountain climbing to chess and piano playing. Like other physicists of his generation, Heisenberg was involved in World War II and the development of the atomic bomb. The details of his role in the bomb's development for Germany are still controversial. After the war, Heisenberg continued his research, traveled widely, and became the director of the Max Planck Institute for Physics in Munich, Germany.

Christiaan Huygens (1629-1695) was born to a wealthy Dutch family in The Hague. Educated in science and mathematics, he was one of many physicists to be puzzled and fascinated by the nature of light. In 1678, Huygens proposed his wave theory of light, which was contrary to the particle theory supported by Newton. It was not until much later that the dual nature of light was discovered. Another of Huygens' great contributions to physics was his study of the pendulum and its applications to timekeeping and clocks. In the field of astronomy, he discovered Saturn's largest moon and more clearly distinguished the shape of Saturn's rings, which were first observed by Italian scientist Galileo. Huygens also had many theories regarding extraterrestrial life and wrote one of the earliest published works on the subject.

James Prescott Joule (1818–1889) was a British physicist. The son of a successful brewer in Manchester, England, Joule was shy and rather sickly as a child. Fortunately, his family's wealth allowed him to be educated at home by private tutors. His science and math teacher was the eminent physicist John Dalton. Joule enjoyed physics and was particularly fascinated by heat and its relationship to energy. He even took time on his honeymoon to measure the temperature difference of water at the top and bottom of a waterfall. He extended his study of heat to include electricity, and he conducted many imaginative and careful experiments in these areas. His work led to the formulation of Joule's law on electric current and resistance. He was also a contributor to the law of conservation of energy.

Antoine-Laurent Lavoisier (1743–1794) was a French chemist who led a rich and busy life. He first studied law, like his father, but he loved science and displayed great talent and energy for research. Recognized as one of the major founders of modern chemistry, Lavoisier was also a dedicated social reformer. As a scientist, he developed a theory of combustion, established a system for naming chemical compounds, and contributed to the law of conservation of matter. As a social activist, he studied ways to improve French agriculture, water quality, public education, and welfare. Unfortunately, Lavoisier's fruitful career was cut short. During the French Revolution's Reign of Terror, he was guillotined for his connection with a tax-collecting agency.

Dmitri Mendeleyev (1834–1907) was born in Siberia, Russia. His early years were rather rocky; when his father went blind, Mendeleyev's mother ran a glass factory to support their large family. A few years later, his father died and the factory burned down. Despite these troubles, Mendeleyev was an excellent student and went to St. Petersburg to study chemistry. Mendeleyev's greatest achievement came about almost by chance. He had created a deck of flash cards, each card showing an atomic element and its properties. He was playing a type of solitaire with the deck when he noticed that, if the cards were laid out in a certain way, elements with similar properties were grouped together. This casual observation led to the creation of Mendeleyev's periodic table.

Albert Michelson (1852–1931) was born in Prussia (modern-day northern Germany), but he and his family moved to the United States when Michelson was four years old. He studied at the Naval Academy in Annapolis, Maryland, and as an officer he taught physics and chemistry. When his duties required him to teach students how to measure the speed of light, he dedicated himself to finding more accurate ways to do so. After leaving the navy, he became a physics professor. The results of his many optical experiments, some done in cooperation with Edward Morley, helped lead to the development of Einstein's theory of relativity. In 1907, Michelson became the first American to receive a Nobel Prize in physics.

Edward Morley (1838–1923) was born in Newark, New Jersey. He began his career as a minister but also studied and taught science. He is probably best known for his work with Albert Michelson measuring the speed of light (the Michelson-Morley experiments). However, Morley was a talented chemist and physicist in his own right. He was especially dedicated to accuracy and precision in his measurements. Much of his work investigated the properties of oxygen. He studied the oxygen content of both air and water and measured the relative atomic mass of oxygen.

Isaac Newton (1642–1727) was born in Woolsthorpe, England. His father, who died a few months before Newton's birth, was a farmer. Newton tried running the family farm, but his talents clearly lay elsewhere—he was a brilliant mathematician and scientist. Just a few of his many important contributions to science include the law of universal gravitation, the three laws of motion, the basic elements of calculus, and the particle theory of light. Newton also served as first the Warden and later the Master of the Mint. In 1705, he was knighted by the queen. He was an unconventional scholar who didn't care much how he looked, and he was often absent-minded. Late in his life, Newton worked less on scientific and mathematical matters, turning instead to the study of alchemy, theology, and history.

Max Planck (1858–1947) was a German physicist who, along with Albert Einstein, developed quantum theory. A brilliant student in many areas, including music, Planck decided to pursue physics as a career and became especially interested in the study of light. His investigations into the frequency and energy of light waves led to his discovery of quanta, the individual packets of energy that make up light. This discovery won him a Nobel Prize and defined the major difference between classical physics and modern physics. In contrast to his great professional success, Planck had a tragic personal life. His wife died after twenty-two years of marriage, one of his sons was killed in World War I, his twin daughters both died in childbirth, and his other son was executed during World War II.

Ernest Rutherford was born in New Zealand. Rutherford was the fourth of twelve children in his family, so money was tight. But Rutherford was an excellent student. In 1895, he won a scholarship to Cambridge University, England, where he worked as a research student for Joseph John (J. J.) Thomson. Rutherford was especially interested in atomic physics and radioactivity, and he did many of the first experiments on the radioactive decay of atoms. However, his most famous work was about the structure of the atom. In 1911, he suggested that atoms contain positively charged particles (protons) which are concentrated in a central, very dense nucleus. Many physicists regard this theory as the beginning of nuclear physics.

Erwin Schrödinger was an Austrian physicist. While serving in the military during World War I, he used his spare time to read books on physics. He was extremely interested in the behavior of atomic particles, especially electrons. In 1926, he presented an equation that described the wavelike properties of orbiting electrons. This theory became known as wave mechanics and is an important part of quantum physics. Schrödinger's work was temporarily interrupted when he left Austria because of Hitler's occupation and the persecution of Jewish people. He traveled to Great Britain, Belgium, Italy, and finally Ireland. He resumed his studies in Ireland and stayed there for seventeen years before returning to Austria to become a professor at the University of Vienna.

Joseph John (J. J.) Thomson was a British physicist who originally intended to be an engineer. However, when his father, a bookseller, died in 1872, Thomson could not afford the fee to become an apprentice. Instead, he decided to study mathematics and physics. After graduating from Trinity College in Cambridge, England, he became a professor there and researched electromagnetism. This work led to his discovery of the electron. Before this time, it was believed that the atom was the smallest unit of matter. Thomson's work led, in turn, to Rutherford's discovery of the proton and the beginnings of nuclear physics. In addition to science, Thomson enjoyed many hobbies. He was a great fan of cricket and rugby, and he especially loved plants and gardening.

Asimov, Isaac. *Asimov's Chronology of Science and Discovery.* New York: HarperCollins, 1994.

Friedhoffer, Robert. *Physics Lab in the Home.* New York: Franklin Watts, 1997.

Henderson, Harry. *Nuclear Physics.* New York: Facts on File, 1998.

Henderson, Harry, and Lisa Yount. *The Scientific Revolution.* San Diego: Lucent Books, 1996.

McPherson, Stephanie Sammartino. *Ordinary Genius: The Story of Albert Einstein.* Minneapolis: Carolrhoda Books, 1995.

Meadows, Jack. *The Great Scientists.* New York: Oxford University Press, 1997.

Severance, John B. *Einstein: Visionary Scientist.* New York: Clarion Books, 1999.

Spangenburg, Ray. *The History of Science from the Ancient Greeks to the Scientific Revolution.* New York: Facts on File, 1993.

Stwertka, Albert. *The World of Atoms and Quarks.* New York: Twenty-First Century Books, 1995.

Wilkinson, Philip, and Michael Pollard. *Scientists Who Changed the World.* New York: Chelsea House Publishers, 1994.

Wood, Robert W. *Who?: Famous Experiments for the Young Scientist.* Philadelphia: Chelsea House Publishers, 1999.

Websites

BBC Online's science site
<http://www.bbc.co.uk/science>

Center for History of Physics, sponsored by the American
  Institute of Physics
<http://www.aip.org/history/index.html>

Cool Science, sponsored by the U.S. Department of Energy
<http://www.fetc.doe.gov/coolscience/index.html>

The Franklin Institute Science Museum online
<http://www.fi.edu/tfi/welcome.html>

Kid's Castle, sponsored by the Smithsonian Institution.
  Includes a science site.
<http://www.kidscastle.si.edu>

NPR's *Sounds Like Science* site
<http://www.npr.org/programs/science>

PBS's *A Science Odyssey* site
<http://www.pbs.org/wgbh/aso>

Science Learning Network
<http://www.sln.org>

Science Museum of Minnesota
<http://www.smm.org/>

For Further Reading

Asimov, Isaac. *Asimov's New Guide to Science.* New York: Basic Books, 1984.

Calder, Nigel. *Einstein's Universe.* New York: Dutton, 1968.

Fisher, David E. *The Ideas of Einstein.* New York: Holt, Rinehart and Winston, 1980.

Galant, Roy A. *Explorers of the Atom.* New York: Doubleday, 1974.

Goldstein-Jackson, Kevin. *Experiments with Everyday Objects: Science Activities for Children, Parents and Teachers.* Englewood Cliffs, NJ: Prentice-Hall, 1978.

Gribbin, John. *In Search of Schrödinger's Cat: Quantum Physics and Reality.* New York: Bantam Books, 1984.

Kent, Amanda, and Alan Ward. *Introduction to Physics.* Tulsa, OK: Usborne Publishing Ltd., 1983.

Kondo, Herbert. *Adventures in Space and Time: The Story of Relativity.* New York: Holiday House, 1966.

Lapp, Ralph E. *Matter.* Life Science Library. New York: Time-Life Books, 1963.

Millar, David, Ian Millar, John Millar, and Margaret Millar. *The Cambridge Dictionary of Scientists.* New York: Cambridge University Press, 1996.

Nourse, Alan E. *Universe, Earth, and Atom: The Story of Physics.* New York: Harper & Row, 1969.

Silverberg, Robert. *Four Men Who Changed the Universe.* New York: G. P. Putnam's Sons, 1968.

Trefil, James. *From Atoms to Quarks: An Introduction to the Strange World of Particle Physics.* New York: Charles Scribner's Sons, 1980.

atom: the tiniest part of a chemical element that has all the properties of that element

conservation of mass/energy, law of: matter is a form of energy. Mass may be converted to energy and energy may be converted to mass. This relationship is described by Einstein's equation $E = mc^2$.

general relativity, Einstein's law of: from a particular point of view, there is no difference between the effects produced by gravitation and acceleration

gravitational lens: a mass large enough to bend light

mass: amount of matter an object or substance is made of

mechanics: the study of motion

photoelectric effect: when light shines on certain metals, an electric current is produced

photons: particles of light

physics: the study of matter and energy and how they behave

Planck's law: the energy of light is directly proportional to its frequency

quantum mechanics: the branch of physics that studies the structure and motion of atoms and subatomic particles

relativity: what you observe and measure about an event depends on your own point of view as well as the event itself

scientific law: a statement that tells how things work in the universe

special relativity, Einstein's law of: the laws of physics are the same for an observer moving at a constant speed as for a stationary observer, and the speed of light is constant for any observer

velocity: the speed of movement in a specific direction

Glossary

About the Author

Paul Fleisher has written more than twenty books for young people and educators, including *Life Cycles of a Dozen Diverse Creatures*, the *Webs of Life* series, and *Brain Food*. His most recent books are *Gorillas* and *Ice Cream Treats: The Inside Scoop*. Paul is a regular contributor to *Technology and Learning* magazine. He has also created several pieces of educational software, including the award-winning *Perplexing Puzzles*.

Paul has taught in Programs for the Gifted in Richmond, Virginia, since 1978. He is also active in civic organizations that work for peace and social justice. In 1988, he received the Virginia Education Association's Award for Peace and International Relations, and in 1999 he was awarded the Thomas Jefferson Medal for Outstanding Contributions to Natural Science Education. In his spare time, you may find Paul walking through the woods, gardening, or fishing on the Chesapeake Bay. Paul and his wife, Debra Sims Fleisher, live in Richmond, Virginia.